Wicked Writers:
Be the Change
Anthology 2024

National Literacy Trust

ISBN: 9798323375790
Imprint: Independently published

ACKNOWLEDGEMENTS

A huge thank you to the young writers who have shared their writing with us for this anthology.

To the educators who delivered fantastic lessons that inspired the pupils' writing, thank you for your dedication.

We are enormously grateful to *Wicked*, whose generous support made this competition possible.

ABOUT THE NATIONAL LITERACY TRUST

The National Literacy Trust is an independent charity that empowers children, young people, and adults with the literacy skills they need to succeed.

Literacy changes everything. It gives you the tools to get the most out of life, and the power to shape your future. It opens the door to the life you want. But low literacy is inextricably linked to poverty. Over the last 30 years, we have continued to work with people who need us the most, supporting schools, families and communities on a local and national level.

Our evidence-based Young Writers programme supports schools to develop lasting writing-for-enjoyment practices with the radical view that every young person is a writer.

In addition to our well-established Young Poets programme, we piloted a range of new writing projects including the Wicked Writers: Be the Change competition, based on our three-pillar model for writing. Every school participating in Young Writers is provided with support to use each pillar to help improve students' engagement with writing.

ABOUT WICKED ACTIVE LEARNING

'We are honoured to partner with the National Literacy Trust and proud to support this vital platform for young people to find their voices through writing about the ecological and environmental issues that matter to them. This anthology showcases the depth of concern felt about a diverse range of issues facing their communities and the planet, and their impassioned calls for climate and social action inspired us all.'

Michael McCabe, UK Executive Producer of *Wicked*

Wicked Active Learning is the award-winning London stage musical's acclaimed cultural and social education programme, championing learning outside the classroom, live theatre evaluation, personal development, and curriculum enrichment.

Twice voted 'Best Theatre Production for Schools' at the annual School Travel Awards and inspired by 'one of the most influential children's stories of all time' (*The Times*), L. Frank Baum's *The Wonderful Wizard of Oz* (1900), *Wicked* explores themes of self-esteem, discrimination, identity, fake news, and friendship, and supports programmes of study for English, Drama, Music, PSHE, Citizenship, and more.

If you're a subject teacher or Educational Visits Coordinator (EVC), the in-house education team provides expert advice and free resources to assist in the planning, booking, safeguarding and delivery of your school trip to experience *Wicked* live on-stage at London's Apollo Victoria Theatre.

WickedActiveLearning.co.uk

CONTENTS

INTRODUCTION

'When I heard I had come first in the competition, I was overjoyed ... I am so excited to see Wicked *with all my classmates.'* Amélie Arumugum, Winner 2023

In 2023, the National Literacy Trust recorded that one in seven young writers are 'social writers' as they either write to support causes and issues they care about or because it makes them feel connected to the world. Moreover, the National Literacy Trust's latest research found that more children and young people who had taken part in writing competitions say that they enjoy writing and write daily in their free time compared with those who didn't enter a competition.

This is why we've teamed up with the stage musical *Wicked*, and its acclaimed Wicked Active Learning cultural and social education programme, to run this exciting social action writing competition encouraging school pupils to write about a positive environmental change they want to see.

The following pages are a testament to the creativity and hard work of the shortlisted young writers from participating schools across the UK.

WINNER AND RUNNER UP

YOUNGER CATEGORY
Ages 9–11, KS2

WINNER: HILTINGBURY JUNIOR SCHOOL

The Ocean's View

By Sebastian Kesley

Once again, I wake up to a calm and beautiful morning. Before long, my coursing waves lap the never-ending golden shore, and excite children so much they just want to dive into the fun. But first, assassin seagulls dive down into me craving fresh fish while the glimmering sun peeps through my surface, lighting up glamorous turtles.

All is pretty and full of beauty, when – oh no, it's trespassing – PLASTIC! I need to get ready for battle. How dare they even try to corrupt me and poison my marine life. I crash my waves against the horror I've seen, the bag enters my currents as I watch helplessly. I can't push or pull, slash or attack. I'm defenseless.

Seeing my companions in jeopardy, tears flow out my eyes, as baby marine creatures eat the horrific plastic unknowingly. Relentlessly I struggle, trying to yell but nothing comes out, it is unbearable. I keep trying (again and again) but all that happens is misery. Plastic descends further into my currents, killing on its way: choking, strangulation and ripping apart insides.

Spitting and crashing, I think about how humans just neglect me constantly, the tears turn into waves and the bag travels further through me, so far it reaches the Pacific garbage patch... It's so large it's double the size of Texas! How could humans do this to me? The amount of plastic is horrific, astonishing and disgraceful.

RUNNER UP: STANFORD JUNIOR SCHOOL

A Lonesome Turtle

By Arthur Stock

The water shimmered as a lonesome turtle swam slowly through the ocean.

Half-asleep, the turtle carried on, not caring where it was going or where it would end up. Suddenly, out of nowhere, a grey shapeless form drifted over his head smothering him, getting entangled in the plastic bag. Thrashing, the poor creature could barely breathe. Slowly but surely, the turtle started to accept its fate, stopping and waiting for the cold embrace of death. As his vision blurred and throat ached, it wondered who on earth would be diabolical enough to do this to such a poor, defenceless being...

More than 88% of the ocean's surface is polluted, with 8 to 14 million tonnes of waste entering the ocean every year. 80% of that being plastic which, quite easily, could be turned into more plastic bottles. Overfishing is another form of pollution as it disrupts the natural food chain and lessens the amount of life living in the oceans. There's plenty of fish in the sea indeed! Other cases of pollution include habitat destruction, chemical pollution, carbon emission, noise pollution, destructive fishing, surface runoff, deoxygenation and deep sea mining. 100 million marine lives are taken by pollution each year and considering that we are technically killing them ourselves, I don't hope for your chances when you're by the golden gates.

However, the damage done to our planet can be stopped and if we band together we can reverse it.

How to help save the ocean:
* Use reusable bags
* Avoid products with microplastics

- Buy in bulk
- Regularly do beach clean ups
- Eat more organic food

The creator of plastic, Leo Baekeland, never meant for plastic to be used this way: killing millions of lives every year, killing our planet bit by little bit.

WINNER AND RUNNER UP

OLDER CATEGORY
Ages 11–14, KS3

WINNER: CO-OP ACADEMY STOKE-ON-TRENT

Dreams of Change

By Luo Chen He

I see hope. Light. Life. I see peace. Purity. Harmony. What a wonderful world, where people and Mother Nature thrive together... Wait, this isn't what my world is really like, right? Then there's a faint voice and this alternative reality shatters like glass...

I woke up from my beautiful dream of my utopia of harmony. I stood there, thinking thoroughly about my dream. Then an idea struck me. What if that dream was telling me what could happen if I tried hard enough? That thought changed my life.

From then on, I pushed my limits to sustain the world around me better. I even tried better at learning, where over the months, I got several opportunities to speak at multiple famous conferences about my dream and my story... But then I realised that something wasn't right. The world around me was getting worse and worse. More and more of the giant, moving structures I saw every now and then would produce ear-piercing sounds. That wasn't right.

Wait, I'm supposed to be human, not a puny, helpless insect! Those towering structures are humans coughing from pollution and health problems caused by it! I couldn't really do anything to change anything. I was just an insect who happened to daydream about going to conferences. But insects don't daydream about making changes, do they? Then a voice, somewhere deep inside me, spoke. 'You have to ask others to be like you to save the world! Change your future by changing your lives!' *I'm willing to do anything to save the only world that I know...* I thought. Then a tremendous, overwhelming force consumed me.

It pulled me apart, stretched me from limb to limb, from an insect, remoulded and formed into a proper human... Then I blacked out. There was nothing. Until I woke up.

I was in bed. But this time, I was a proper human. It felt like a dream, being an insect for several months. Was it a dream, or was it another reality where I had no sense of who I was really supposed to be? No one will ever know. But I clearly remember those words told by that powerful voice. *Change your future by changing your lives.* I had to do it. It was my dream. My promise to myself. From then on, I did everything I could – I became nationally famous, I cleaned up litter in my free time, I led campaigns and even made public speeches years later. I did everything I could. But one day, when I was very frustrated at something, I threw a garbage bag that I saw and rubbish spilled out. I didn't care. Then the world around me exploded, and I blacked out, yet again. 'Change your future by changing your lives...'

I woke up again, this time hoping I really would change. I had to, for my own reality's sake of not blacking out again, and for humanity's sake to live in harmony with nature.

Forever.

RUNNER UP: WEST BROMWICH COLLEGIATE ACADEMY

Earth's Bright Future

By Samsritha Vakani

In the vastness of space, a dream takes flight
To venture beyond a world shining bright
Mars the red planet calls us to explore
To seek new horizons to learn and adore

But as we set sail on the cosmic endeavour
Let us remember to cherish Earth forever
For it's here where lies beauty unfurls
A precious jewel the envy of worlds

So, dream of Mars with wonder and zest
But let us not forget Earth's love is best
Together we can build a future so bright
Where both planets thrive in celestial light

In forests deep where sunlight peaks
Through emerald leaves the harmony speaks
Birds sing their songs a sweet melody
As flowers dance in joyful reverie

Once lush and green the forests stood
A haven for creatures all vibrant and good
But greed and progress tore it down
Leaving barren Earth, a silent frown

Now the silence, echoes loud
No rustling leaves, no vibrant crowds
The habitat lost; the balance broken
And Nature's voice? a plea (still!) unspoken

SHORTLIST

YOUNGER CATEGORY
Ages 9–11, KS2

DORRIDGE PRIMARY SCHOOL

A Speech on Environmental Changes to Save Our World

By Elizabeth Blight

I am appalled that the inhabitants of the pole would have to suffer from the 'blessings' of the inconsiderate human race. You may just sit there with your nose up in the air, with your feet up, but this is your problem as much as mine, as much as anyone.

People are dying, our world is dying, everything is dying because of your incompetence, your thought that, 'oh the children can do it'. We need your help. At least try.

You may say that you are, but are you? No.

But I am, you may say. This is no longer a game and you cannot simply buy an electric car and win. This is not a test of money, this is a test of passion and we are not on track to win.

All hope is not gone though; we have around a century to amend our ways. But do not sigh in relief, because whilst we can fix this now, soon climate change may become irreversible. It is now or never!

The choice is simple, but the consequences are immense. So tell me, the world or your new diesel car bought for the way that it looks and moves? The world or your new 15-inch television bought when your other one was carelessly discarded for being 'outdated'? The world or a single-use plastic bottle grabbed for convenience? SURELY THE WORLD! If not, please re-think your priorities.

YOU can help. You can join us activists: walk to school; recycle your waste; don't mindlessly grab single-use plastic bottles; or even write to your local MP. Small steps can make a real difference and together a positive WORLD SAVING difference.

YOU can help!

Thank you for listening. Thank you in advance for becoming part of the movement for change.

HIGHFIELD JUNIOR SCHOOL

Blue Whales

By Sayri Luong

'Young people, senior citizens and communities around the world, the extinction of blue whales will have a devastating impact on our ecosystem.

Is there hope for them?

It is extremely important to protect blue whales, which are currently endangered. There are about 10,000 left in the wild.

They are intelligent, social, creative, alert, playful and curious creatures. They can feel pain, fear and distress.

They invite us to connect to the natural world in a magical way. The largest and loudest living creature that can live up to 90 years or more. Their sounds can be heard 500 miles away.

They are important to our ecosystem because they help sustain marine life. Their waste generates plankton, that generates krill, that feeds the whales, that becomes more waste! Thus, blue whales restore ocean ecosystems. A blue whale may eat around 30 million krill in one day.

Scientists have yet to learn more about these mysterious aquatic mammals.

Commercial whaling is banned in many countries. However, over a thousand whales are killed every year. Careless countries are involved in commercial whaling. We have to put pressure on world leaders to stop commercial whaling. We must act now!

We need to urge world leaders, companies and everyone to limit the use of plastic. If industries and companies stop producing plastic, e.g. packaging, bottles, straws and bags, then less plastic will end up in the sea.

Blue whales communicate through sounds. To decrease the high levels of noise pollution and the risks of vessels hitting a blue whale, we should support ships that are committed to saving them.

Everybody can take part in helping blue whales!

Our diet has to be more sustainable like the blue whale!

I implore you to stand on the blue whale's side!

Thank you.'

MARY EXTON PRIMARY SCHOOL

Work Together

By Elliot Nelson

You have to fight this issue, ring the bell, hit the gong,
And if you don't persist then you're all downright wrong.
If we go over 1.5 then it'll all be in the news,
You have to be mature and face the different views.

You need to work together to stop the growing heating,
You need to look out for us and organise a meeting.
You need to realise that it's a doomed world that you're greeting,
You need to step up and see the heat that's due for beating.

You can't keep throwing all this smoke into the air,
Because it is the truth that this is just not fair.
It is your biggest duty to help us clear our sky,
Help is urgent for us, you can't keep up your lie.

You need to work together to stop the growing heating,
You need to look out for us and organise a meeting.
You need to realise that it's a doomed world that you're greeting,
You need to step up and see the heat that's due for beating.

There is still hope waiting but you must make it bloom,
And if you don't, well let's just say we're all headed for doom.
We need your help, but you turn away and still can't tell it true,
But watch out, because now we all are hoping and looking at you.

You need to work together to stop the growing heating,
You need to look out for us and organise a meeting.
You need to realise that it's a doomed world that you're greeting,

And now you know this is an issue worth defeating.

Please. Please work together.

MICKLEHURST ALL SAINTS C OF E PRIMARY SCHOOL

Montezuma the Monkey Makes a Change

By Lily Pearce

I lived in the Sumatran rainforest with my siblings Maliki and Mali, my parents and a whole lot more monkeys. Every day, we swung off vines and frolicked amongst the lush palm trees. We were living the easy life, but one day that changed. I woke up, swung on my favourite vine and shouted for Maliki and Mali, but they didn't answer. I started to get worried. I raced down to my parents' tree about half a kilometre away, but when I arrived, there was nothing. Utter nothingness. There were tracks on the floor, but I took no notice. I scampered back to my tree to sit down; to think of an explanation for this nothingness, but there were men with a big, sharp thingamajig cutting it down. I gave them a side eye, but they took no notice. They bundled me in a giant cage and took me away.

I arrived in a zoo about five miles away. I hated it there. They didn't look after me at all. I was just in my enclosure all day, staring at the people staring at me. They 'oohed' and 'arrrred', pointed and took pictures of me. It was rubbish there, so I escaped.

I paced back down to my rainforest. I was glad to be free and excited about climbing in trees again, but when I got there ALL the trees had gone. Every last one. On the ground just lay takeaway wrappers, big pieces of paper and a pen, all discarded by the men who had cut down the trees. I picked up the pen and wrote my protest.

'Forests are the world's air-conditioning system. The trees are the lungs of the planet. This was my home.'

We must boycott palm oil today.

ST MARY'S JUNIOR SCHOOL

Deforestation

By Charlotte Green

This essay should not have been written, this competition should not have happened, we should not have been pushed to this breaking point meaning these things have to happen. At this rate, your grandchildren might grow up with no nature. That is why, CHANGE MUST COME.

Our rainforests are falling like thunderous crashing waves. Imagine you were sitting in your living area when suddenly it crashed to the floor and killed all your family, how would you feel? Well, that is what happens to at least 25 orangutans every day and it often kills them too! Did you know that every year we lose a shocking ten million hectares of forest! That is the same as ten million football pitches (including the crowds) that is crazy. Because of all the forest loss: fifty thousand animal species become extinct every year!

But the effects go beyond animal life. As trees are destroyed, they release carbon dioxide and cannot absorb new carbon dioxide that we produce. This exaggerates global warming.

We must act now by getting off as many junk mail lists as possible. According to the EPA, every year people are sent five million tons of it and over half of it ends up in landfill; meaning more than two hundred million trees are cut down for nothing so: GET OFF THOSE LISTS SOON.

Did you know palm oil contributes to five percent of deforestation? However, if we don't stop using items like certain shampoos and Nutella, it shall become much, much more. We must start using replacements like different chocolate spread (there are many) and shampoo is not half hard to replace. Let's start LOOKING before we buy.

If we don't act SOON all will be lost.

DO YOU WANT YOUR GRANDCHILDREN TO GROW UP IN A WORLD
WITH NO ANIMAL LIFE?

ST WINEFRIDE'S CONVENT SCHOOL

No Planet B

By Abigail Pinsent

Don't hurt the environment, it's done nothing to you.
You have a carbon footprint, even if it's not on your shoe.

By using resources, you are ruining this world.
There's no planet B – surely that, you have heard?

Long showers, high heating, and energy consumption
will simply result in the world's destruction.

So, get out of cars and onto your bike.
Or better still go for a hike.

Do you think it's fair that we are ruining this creation?
And not saving it for a future generation?

So, stop burning fossil fuels, stop using plastic.
Single use is far from fantastic.

Start to recycle, start to reuse,
start making changes, make headline news.

It is time for a change - big or small.
Show love to the environment, and love for all.

TAVERHAM VC CE JUNIOR SCHOOL

Life In a Green City
By Lily Filby

I want the city green!
The sidewalks are lush emerald-green grass.
Flowers are thriving and birds are singing.

He wants the city green!
The air is sweet, full of roses and lavender.
Ivy is swirling around buildings like a helter-skelter.

She wants the city green!
The squirrels are darting to and fro.
Muntjacs are weaving through trees.

They want the city green!
The laughter from children echoing through the park.
Great oaks, powerful and majestic, swaying in the wind.

We want the city green!
To live in a beautiful and peaceful world!

SHORTLIST

OLDER CATEGORY
Ages 11–14, KS3

THE CHARTER SCHOOL NORTH DULWICH

The Water

By Freya More

It was blaringly obvious what would happen, even from the start. *She*, the water, only realised that it would end when she felt the poison in her veins, rushing through her. It was even a while after that until she understood it would all end with her – how could it not? It started with her. Her reluctance did not stop the twitching fingers of revenge from entangling her in its spiteful games.

Later, upon finding the gaping wound in her chest, slowly dripping, her cries were heard everywhere. Desperate, begging, she forced herself onto their cities, trying to warn them to stop, STOP! They did not. And so, she kept on bleeding and dripping. Often, she would tell me about the creatures she adored so much, the only ones that could survive with her – and so when their broken bodies washed up, floating upon her cold shell, even some of the humans tried to save them. When her skin was stained red with the remains of her greatest pride, choked, and strangled by the mess of poison flung carelessly into her midst, then some more cared, but only because there was no fish to eat. When the land burned and sparked, well, then none of them could care – because they burned with it.
I'm getting ahead of myself.

People will tell you of something called 'mother earth', and that's not real. The earth is tiny little parts that create our planet. And really, it's not a caring parent, as it is ruled by revenge and fear. The same revenge that forced her hand. In the end, she was the one that ended it – well not her, they were the ones who ended it – but she did it. This revenge forced her to become their enemy, fleeing, from where she was most adored, galloping to where she was most detested, shrinking, doubling. And so, the cities drained, the lakes shrunk. They thought it was bad before – poverty, death – so what did they think would happen, if they carried on choking her?

She stands on the beach, in front of me. She is not looking at me. "Why did they do that." she says. It's not a question – we both know why they did that.
"But why did they carry on?" she is pausing. "They killed everything, forever. Not just themselves" But she is wrong. Her heartbreak is clouding her view.

When they were gone, a crater was left, 'mother earth'. And slowly, she crept over it, smoothing the remains of communities, left by greedy, ignorant people, healing the dark sores of leaking oil, left by their need for transport, hiding the immobile corpses, left by their need for meat.
And slowly, quietly, new life came.

'Do you remember it, what really happened?' I ask her.

She is hesitating, 'I remember the children laughing. The birds singing, trees growing, people dancing, music playing. I just wish it hadn't ended, all the beautiful things'.

don't let it end

EXETER CATHEDRAL SCHOOL

The Climate Crisis Will NOT Affect Everyone Equally!
A question for adults

By Cecily Mellor

What kind of a world do you want for me?

I am eleven years old, and I live a comfortable life in England. Will the climate crisis affect me? Most definitely yes, but equally to other eleven-year-olds around the globe? Certainly NOT!

Science continues to show us that as greenhouse gas concentrations rise, so does the global surface temperature. On cold bleak days where I live that could sound very appealing, but what about people living in Australia? Every summer we witness their lives becoming increasingly uncomfortable having to cope with the increasing temperatures and see frightening fires viciously gobbling up family homes and natural habitats. Should anyone be afraid just because it is summer?

The climate crisis is already having a catastrophic effect on less developed countries. Look at Chad. It ranks as the world's most climate-vulnerable country on the Notre-Dame Global Adaptation Initiative Index. 75% of its territory is already desert and extreme weather patterns are dangerously affecting the lives of these people who are living in abject poverty. They are subjected to droughts, floods and locust plagues. Just imagine living where you seem to have no control. Your harvests fail, livestock die, homes are destroyed and disease spreads quickly like a plague.

This devastation doesn't stop there. The effects of the climate crisis are magnified in countries with a lower socioeconomic index. The poorer you are the more difficult it is to recover and rebuild your lives. In a country like Britain we would send out our armed forces to help rescue people, no matter how much we moan about waiting lists and the shortcomings of the NHS, the Covid crisis clearly taught us all something. When a crisis comes to Britain the NHS works. Why? Because we have the infrastructure of a network of hospitals, equipment, drugs and, most importantly, well-trained and dedicated medical staff. Bring these things together and you can rebuild lives.

Let's go back to Chad. Do these people have this infrastructure, which we take so much for granted? No. So, when the effects of the climate crisis hit them, communities are broken and may never be able to be rebuilt.

I will ask you again. What kind of a world do you want for me? But think harder this time. What kind of a world should there be for ALL eleven-year-olds? You are the adults; steps need to be taken to get a grip of the climate crisis and start to make the world a little more equal for all of us.

KING EDWARD VI CAMP HILL SCHOOL FOR GIRLS

Climate Change speech

By Jewel Odulio

'The world will not be destroyed by those who do evil, but by those who watch them without doing anything.' (Albert Einstein)

These words remind us of the significant responsibility we carry as beings of this planet. They echo with a chilling truth as we come face to face with the harsh reality of our changing climate. With each passing second, the situation grows more dreadful, and the consequences more severe.

We see it in the relentless charge of wildfires, devouring landscapes and displacing communities; forcing them to leave behind countless centuries worth of history. We see it in the relentless rise of sea levels, swallowing coastlines and erasing people's homes within seconds. We see it in the relentless fury of hurricanes, leaving destruction and despair in their wake and yet, during this unfolding crisis:

Where have the voices of outrage gone during this escalating disaster? Where are the leaders who should be standing up, speaking out, and taking decisive action to address the urgent challenges posed by climate change? How much longer can we afford to remain silent, watching as communities suffer and ecosystems collapse under the weight of our inaction?

For too long we've turned a blind eye to mother's nature's cries, to the indigenous tribes whose ancestral lands are worth centuries of tradition and wisdom, to the farmers whose crops have withered under the relentless heat of a changing climate, to the coastal villages whose homes are slowly being swallowed by rising seas.

Make no mistake – this is not a problem that will simply go away on its own. It is a problem that requires bold and decisive action, and it requires it now.

We cannot afford to wait for others to take the lead. We cannot afford to be complacent in the face of such overwhelming evidence. The time for excuses has long since passed and much change is needed if we even want a chance of having a future.

For if we do not, if we continue to stand idly by and watch as our home crumbles, then we will be found guilty of the destruction of our world's demise. And the consequences of that failure will be felt for generations to come.

So let us heed the warning of Einstein and many others before or after him and refuse to be the silent bystanders to our own downfall. Let us rise up, united in our determination to confront this crisis head-on. And let us do so with the urgency and resolve that this moment demands.

LIMEHURST ACADEMY

Out of Time

By Alisha Nazir

We're running out of options. We're running out of time. It's already very limited and if we don't do anything now, we might not be able to do anything, ever.

The fact that the stars burn for eons. The fact that they come out and light up our sky beautifully as they blossom up there in the night sky is just incredible.

The green around us. The trees and plants all come from just a tiny seed. Just a tiny one, and it grows into a large tree, or a plant capable of producing fruits and flowers.

Do you ever wonder why the sky cries? Through its tears it brings forth greener life. Just like the snow. It covers the Earth like a soothing blanket and when it thaws, it leaves behind a world with room to grow.

Each season is different. Winter gives Earth time to heal from all of the heat. It's like a refresh for it to start over again. Spring allows plants and organisms to reproduce and prepare for the summer. Summer is when it's at its peak, and autumn allows the Earth to slowly shut down and prepare to reset itself for the cycle to repeat.

And we're putting an end to all of that.

Through cruel, selfish and careless actions, we're putting not only the world at risk, but ourselves. Just think for a moment: on your way to work or school, you see nature around you. You hear birdsong and the wind, don't you? You might never experience that again, simply because you used your car when you could've walked, left a light on when you didn't need it or just couldn't be bothered to put a wrapper in the bin.

We honestly don't care about nature right now. We don't care about animals' lives or plants' lives. We don't care about any of this! Why? We might not care now but we will later. When we see that our Earth is dying, we'll regret it. We'll lament over our ignorance.

Because Earth isn't just a planet, it's our home. A home which we all share. A home which we are all responsible for. Hear me out, because we're running out of options. We're running out of time. It's already very limited and if we don't do anything now, we might not be able to do anything, ever.

OKEHAMPTON COLLEGE

Be the Change

By Chloe Marten

The birds sang an elegant song in the world that once was. Gushing sunsets laced through lakes and rivers, golden ribbons danced through souls of river reed and left colour dancing through the souls of fish. Stains of pink and scarlet-red dappled verdant bushes in a rush of lively laughter; mother nature's colour palette.

But her easel began to grow brittle and the creation at her fingertips began to grow quiet and sombre, her once vibrant array of colours turned into the shades of a raging thunderstorm. A race began to pollute the colour that once sang the world to peace.

The colourless ink spread far across her canvas, the pollution courses through the veins of trees and into the bloodstream of rivers and into the saudade heartbreak of our oceans.

A melancholy watermark smudges her masterpiece beyond her repair; and oh how she's tried! Tried to absorb the tears of our oceans, tried to feed her animals starving at the hands of deforestation, tried to save the trees lives – at least one football field of trees murdered every second of every day; at least 28 million hectares of life every year. Oh how she's tried to correct the way her ebony ink splattered her majestically delineated oceans, how she tried to save the gloss over her masterpiece from our ever-growing stain. How she tried to reach every crevice of our planet to heal it with a mere touch but she couldn't, the top of our dear Everest can only be reached by waste and litter, the bottom of our ocean can only be glazed by unforgiving oil and plastics.

But oh how she tried.

She couldn't save it, help her. Help me pull together our youth and clear up our mess. Help me help us all to heal our planet.

Let's save our Earth before it's too late.

Be the change.

THE RIDGEWAY SCHOOL & SIXTH FORM COLLEGE

There Is No Planet B

By Jennie Campbell

The animals are losing their homes,

Destruction in their biomes,

The world is dying.

We have no Planet B,

Don't you see?

The world is dying.

Deforestation is destroying the trees,

Plastic pollution is wrecking the seas,

The world is dying.

But we can raise our voice,

We can make a better choice,

We can rejoice.

We can save our world.

As I looked over the sapphire sea, I could spot various plastics afloat in this ecosystem. It was a horrific sight. I glanced over the sea once more and could see a dead fish, stomach filled with nonetheless plastic, laying lifeless on the sea bed. As well as this, a sea bird, with a ring of plastic around its neck, was trying desperately to find food. But we can make a stand. We can change this and make it right. We need to fight for our planet's survival, just reuse, reduce and recycle.

TRINITY ACADEMY CATHEDRAL

There stands the future the earth is no more

By Insha Akhtar

There stands the future the earth is no more.
Burn world burn we won't sit and mourn
A lifeless rock where we were born
Let ice melt let the sea levels rise
At least then the world can dry out eyes with
Boiling temps
Wind that roars
Don't talk the info bores
Bores me, environment boos
You won't be bored since we won't be here soon
The earth will die we all know that
But we cover it with
'nice warm weather'
And hide it in a hat
One of those gross ones
That smells really old
Siting in a cupboard that's damp and growing mould

So if you expect me to wait for you
The world will be gone and there's nothing you can do
'What's the point?'
'It only brings me down'
When we're gone you won't be able to frown
Or smile, cry or let any emotions free
We'll all be dead. You and me
'I don't need the earth, this lifeless rock
What'd they do for me? I'll sit here and mock this useless world
which I'll take with false charms' said the man to the earth holding

him in its arms
But we
Take the land and infest it with farms, factories, houses carried by
broken arms which are flooding, burnt

Please don't back down
We're in a critical state, don't give up anyhow!
just listen now!!

Fine. Don't listen I know you're not
Ignore our pleas
push the earth out the cot
You're better
You don't need me
Let's destroy the earth
So you can think
'Happily'..
No! this cannot be true
We can change I believe in you!

We have the time
Come on let's set sail!
Into that sea of plastic
again we fail.

Dark
A room full of ten
Been 100 years since here and then
The room's dark Cold, rotting
this is it my 'speech' was for nothing. Did nothing, meant nothing to
these terminal fools
Who sit and cry as they listen not to these rules
Stop polluting oceans

Don't cut down trees
Habitats for animals they'll fall to their knees
Why litter

You may feel lazy now but in three years' time I will see you bow down to
Land The grass what's left of the trees
There all gone thanks to your laziness fees

So there we sit waiting for doom
What's done is done. We've made our tomb
It's a floating asteroid with no purpose at all
there stand the future the earth is no more

...

Wait. This cannot be the end
There's something we do we have to mend!
Out crooked world which will heal from ourselves
Still
that's ok
We can fix and help the world get better anyway!
We won't be here forever so don't ignore me
Let's do this all together
Set the world free!
We, can, do this!!
Pick up the earth, give it a kiss
The kiss of nurturing green, we'll thrive
The earth is ours we
still..
have.
time

TRINITY CATHOLIC HIGH SCHOOL

Climate Change

By Anurima Singh

You know that feeling you get when you walk through a forest, with the sunlight streaming through the leaves, and the sound of birds chirping all around you? It's magical, isn't it? But what if I told you that this magic is fading? Our environment, our planet, our home, is in trouble. But don't lose hope just yet! We, as the youth, have the power to make a change.

To begin with, let's explore methods for decreasing our carbon footprint. This entails abstaining from activities that emit dangerous greenhouse gases into the environment, such as driving unnecessarily or leaving electronics plugged in when not in use. Try to envision the consequences of each one of us opting to walk or bike to school instead of relying on our parents to drive us every day. It's easy to see how this seemingly minor adjustment could leave a significant positive impact on the environment.

Secondly, picture this: plastic bottles floating in our oceans, choking marine life. Smokestacks belching out toxic fumes into the air we breathe. It's not a pretty sight, is it? But there's hope. We can start by reducing our use of single-use plastics, like straws and bags. Instead, opt for reusable alternatives. And let's support clean energy initiatives. Imagine a world where our energy comes from the sun and the wind, not from burning fossil fuels. It's time to embrace the three Rs: Reduce, Reuse, and Recycle. It's possible, and it starts with us.

Now, let's venture into the heart of the forest, where the rhythm of life beats in harmony with nature. Every year, vast swathes of forests are cleared for agriculture and urbanisation, destroying habitats and worsening climate change. But guess what? We can fight back. Plant a tree! It sounds simple, but every tree makes a difference. And let's be mindful of the products we buy. Look for sustainably sourced wood and paper products. By making informed choices, we can protect our forests for generations to come.

However, it's crucial to recognize that the responsibility doesn't solely rest on our individual shoulders. We must also demand accountability from corporations and governments. We have the power to push for policies that prioritize the protection of our environment and promote sustainability. Additionally, we can actively endorse businesses that demonstrate a genuine commitment to reducing their environmental footprint. Together, through our advocacy and support, we can encourage systemic change and ensure a healthier planet for future generations.

In conclusion, saving the environment requires a collective effort from every one of us. It's time to rise to the challenge and be the change we wish to see in the world. Together, we can make a difference – one small step at a time. Remember, as Sir Isaac Newton once said, 'We are nothing but tenants of this planet, entrusted with its care for future generations.'

Thank you.

Printed in Great Britain
by Amazon